# MAHAMUDRA

The Poetry of the Mahasiddhas

Translation and Introduction
by
Keith Dowman

Dzogchen Now! Books

2020

A *Dzogchen Now!* Book
www.keith.dowman@gmail.com

© Keith Dowman 2020

All rights reserved. No part of this book may be reproduced in any form or by any means, electronic or mechanical, including photography, recording, or by any information storage or retrieval system or technologies now known or later developed without permission in writing from the publisher.

ISBN-: 9781660775941

Printed in the U.S.A.
Font set in Baskerville 10.5

## CONTENTS

Introduction  7

Saraha's Dohakosha  The King's Song  15

Saraha's Dohakosha  The Queen Doha  21

Saraha's Charyagiti  29

Nakpopa's Dohakosha  31

Tilopa's Mahamudra Instruction to Naropa  33

Tilopa's Dohakosha  39

Naropa's Concise Mahamudra View  41

Virupa's Dohakosha  47

Maitripa's Essential Mahamudra Verses  55

The Life of the Master Tilopa  57

Appendix  79

# Introduction

'Mahamudra', insists Tilopa, 'cannot be taught', and Mahamudra reigns supreme in the Tibetan Buddhist firmament. Buddhism with its sutras and tantras and innumerable commentaries, explanatory and philosophical, can definitely be taught. Buddhism is learned on a graduated path, but Mahamudra is intuited on an immediate or pathless path. Whether Mahamudra can be reached – as the contemporary Kahgyu tradition would have it – through graduated training, is a moot point. The original Mahamudra literature represented here by the *dohakoshas* and additional material of its Indian lineage undoubtedly affirms its instantaneous nature. Or rather, it affirms the instantaneous nature of our realisation of it, for Mahamudra is not something that comes and goes or is capable of being attained or lost – it is a constant, the only constant, in an ever-changing universe of illusion. Whether we are aware of it or not, it is the air that we breathe, the stuff of our every perception, the bodymind that perceives, the awareness inherent in our consciousness and our every thought.

How can Mahamudra be a constant and simultaneously the stream of ever-changing sensory perception and internal mentation? What is Mahamudra when it is both appearance and emptiness? The answer is that sensory perception never separates from the constant that is Mahamudra. This is the conundrum that is perpetrated in the dohakoshas. The word 'sunyata' is widely used in Mahamudra exposition, and the notion of 'maya', the illusory nature of all experience – thought and perception – is fundamental, but Mahamudra itself, as pristine cognition, is nondual. As such it cannot be attained, but then again, it cannot be lost: in this way it is the 'natural state'.

The dohakoshas focus on the ineffable quality of the natural state, the impossibility of grasping it, its utter transcendence of the intellect, and assume that in the resultant intuitive/nonfunctional letting go, the nondual state will come into its own. The dohas do not dwell on that inexpressible state – for obvious reasons. The notion of transcendent compassion, although incipient, is not therefore dwelt upon. The dohas' purpose is to incite the realisation of what is already present; compassion is the inevitable and automatic result of that realisation and may be seen in the siddhas' songs of realisation.

The doha couplets and verses that express Mahamudra, originating with the Indian Mahamudra mahasiddhas, are probably the best poetic expression of Mahamudra. However, when Mahamudra reached Tibet and became *chakya chembo*, it became subject to the logical scholarly Tibetan mind that insists upon dissecting every 'doctrine' under the four categories of academic analysis: view, meditation, action and result. In this verbal frame, or something similar, the original joy, or ecstasy, of Mahamudra attainment has come down to us.

The principal contemporary holders of the Mahamudra tradition are the various subschools of the Kahgyu tradition, particularly the Drukpa and the Karma Kahgyu. These schools are adept in the language of nonduality, an accomplishment difficult to master in European languages that have so little history of it. This linguistic privation shows itself in the tendency to designate nondual experience in a negative light, as an absence, rather than a fullness, as nothingness rather than a nondual something. Nondual experience may lack objectification but not necessarily 'heart'.

*Mahamudra and Dzogchen*

In a generalized Western perspective the Mahamudra and Dzogchen traditions are equal in outcome as buddha, and looking with a yogin's eyes the Dzogchen Mahamudra views are existentially or experientially very similar. Like Dzogchen, Mahamudra transcends the mind and all thought about it, and like Dzogchen it assumes an absence of conceptual objectification; and yet all thought is embraced in its all-inclusive scope. In this way Mahamudra and Dzogchen are both terms for experiential nondual reality, and about that nothing definitive can be said.

In practical terms, in Kahgyu school praxis, Mahamudra requires a demanding preliminary course of meditation, and that gives it a graduated appearance. Moreover, in Dzogchen exegesis, Mahamudra indicates only a partial attainment, and indeed may be understood conceptually as the female principle, the Great Mother; it is associated with the Secret Empowerment and sexual consummation; it is also explicated among the four mudras: karmamudra, samayamudra, dharmamudra and mahamudra. In this way, as a positive experience, Mahamudra is subsumed by Dzogchen.

In another perspective, Mahamudra and Dzogchen are equal but quite distinct. In their poetic expression they utilise quite different modes and vocabularies. The Mahamudra doha versification originating in eastern India has no comparison with anything originated in the North-west. Another facet of doha expression is the use of simile and metaphor, features which are rare in Dzogchen expression. Although the Dzogchen and Mahamudra views are virtually indistinguishable, the differences in style between the two traditions can provide the leverage that determines to which a Western yogin/yogini turns.

*About the poet-authors*
Saraha is given first place in the works of the Mahamudra siddhas because he represents an original source of Mahamudra which otherwise is lost in the hoary past of Indian history. Iconographically Saraha holds an arrow, his symbolic accoutrement, and is labelled 'the Archer', but in his legend amongst the eighty-four mahasiddhas there is no mention of Saraha as an archer. His Guru may have been Haribhadra and his principal disciple Nagarjuna and he may have lived in the early tenth century, but what is certain is that he figured principally in the lineage of the *Chakrasambara* and *Hevajra-tantras*, and that his lineal successors were also links in that lineage. Although our knowledge of the lineage is still mostly derived from legend, it appears that Saraha and his successors thrived during the royal Pala hegemony in Bengal from the 8th-11th century.

The poet-siddhas under whose names these Mahamudra teaching-verses were composed are counted among the eight-four mahasiddhas: Saraha, Nakpopa, Tilopa, Naropa, Virupa and Maitripa. 'According to tradition, these were renunciate yogins, mendicant sadhu-yogins, living with the people on a grass-roots level of society, teaching more by psychic vibration, posture and attitude – mantra, mudra and tantra – than by sermonising. Some of these siddhas were iconoclasts, dissenters and anti-establishment rebels fulfilling the necessary function of destroying the rigidity of old and intractable customs and habits, so that spontaneity and new vitality could flourish. Obsessive caste rules and regulations in society, and religious ritual as an end in itself, were undermined by the siddhas' exemplary free-living. The irrelevance of scholastic hair-splitting in an academic language, together with a host of social and religious evils, were exposed in the poets' wonderful mystical songs written in their vernacular tongue. They taught existential involvement rather than metaphysical speculation, and they taught the ideal of living in the world but not of it rather than ascetic self-mutilation or monastic renunciation. The siddhas are characterised by a lack of external uniformity and formal discipline...

'Those siddhas who became most renowned – Luipa, Saraha, Tilopa, Naropa and Virupa – who initiated lineages that, through Tibet, are still alive today, were renunciate yogins who abandoned home and family ties, their palaces and academies, security and comfort, fame and wealth, and the institutional fabric of existence, to practice in conditions of deprivation. All eighty-four performed the same alchemical meditations...'

The siddhas represented here – Saraha, Nakpopa, Tilopa, Naropa Virupa and Maitripa – appear late in the siddha galaxy, but were undoubtedly the root of the Tibetan Mahamudra lineage. To obsess with their succession in the lineage is pointless insofar as there is no development in their exposition of Mahamudra. The renowned association between Tilopa and Naropa is the exception, because it provides a paradigm of the supra-rational and existential Mahamudra guru-disciple relationship. The down-to-earth human aspect is alluded to in the dohas but the overwhelming tenor of the verses is highly abstract/intellectual, and although compared to Dzogchen exegesis this Mahamudra is laced with concrete metaphor and simile, still it is hardly the language of wild and woolly sadhus.

The legend of Tilopa that has been included here after the verses represents him not only as a Mahamudra exemplar and a pandita who can defeat accomplished Hindu extremists, but primarily as a siddha-magician capable of the supra-rational manifestation that characterises the Mahamudra lineage down the centuries. In Tibet, it is represented particularly by Milarepa. Marpa and Rechungpa. Our principal source of information about the mahasiddhas is Abhayadatta Sri's *Legends of the Mahasiddha*. Those legends provide a historical and cultural background to the siddha's milieu beside multiple examples of the form of creative and fulfilment stage instruction on the graduated Mahamudra path. Tilopa's life-story on the contrary, although the graduated path is allowed, shows Mahamudra as a transcendent, timeless odyssey, on an immediate instantaneous path.

*About the form of the doha verses*
The original Tibetan verses were labelled 'dohas' which requires some explanation. The doha refers to a two-line metrical verse form used primarily in the sanskritized *apabhramsa* dialect current in the north-east of India (Bengal) during the centuries before the Turkic invasions, which began in the 11th century. Mahamudra burgeoned in this part of India during the Pala and Sena dynasties (9th-13th centuries) which − most unusually − were Buddhist in their religious affinity. In Tibet the word *doha* lost its original meaning and came to describe the versified poetic literature of Mahamudra which the early Mahamudra lineage-holders spoke and sang. More specifically it defines the verses of Tibetan translation of Mahamudra material translated from those Apabhramsa sources. In the English translation no trace whatsoever of the original doha form remains.

The original doha form, however, was in metrical couplets ideal for transmitting the mnemonic aphorisms containing the essential wisdom of Mahamudra. In Tibetan translation the metrical form was lost, but the 'doha' tag remained in the label 'doha mdzod' (dohakosha), which is best translated as 'doha-treasury' or 'cache of aphorisms', which is the title shared by most of the eight scriptures composing the pecha. These 'doha mdzod' texts could be understood as collections of Mahamudra aphorisms collated by a Tibetan translator or editor under appropriate headings and assigned to an appropriate Bengali author with high lineal standing. A Sakya school editor would have had access to the library of the principal Sakya gompa, located not far from the Nepali border, which held a treasure trove of Apabhramsa texts. The doha treasury of Virupa, for example, may have been assembled from the fragmentary material attributed to the mahasiddha and lineage holders or his disciples in such texts. The headings and subheads were undoubtedly a Tibetan device probably inserted for easy learning and assimilation by Tibetan acolytes. The doha form, the prerogative of the yogins of eastern India, was translated into Tibetan in a mnemonic verse form unknown in the Indian North-west.

*About the original pecha texts*
The dohakoshas of Tilopa, Naropa, Virupa, Nakpopa and Maitripa are to be found in a small volume of Tibetan texts printed from woodblocks kept at the Gyelwa Karmapa's monastery at Rumtek, Sikkim. The blockprint is entitled *Eight Doha Treasuries: An Enlightening Collection of Mahamudra Pith Precepts* (*Do ha mdzod brgyad ces bya ba Phyag rgya chen po'i man ngag gsal bar ston pa'i gzhung*). The blockprint was also available at the Drukpa Kahgyu gompa at Tashi Jong in the Kangra Valley, Himachal Pradesh, India. When in 1967, Mario Maglietti and I, together with friends arrived at Tashi Jong and requested Mahamudra instruction from His Holiness Khamtrul Rinpoche, this was the text he gave us, and from which he taught on successive days. Khamtrul Rinpoche Dongyu Nyima (1931-1980) founded the eastern Tibetan Khampagar Monastery in exile in the Tashi Jong community in the early 1960s and played a leading role in reviving the Drukpa Kahgyu dharma.

*About the translation*
The translation from Apabhramsa to Tibetan was made by an Indian called Berotsana, which is a Tibetan form of sanskritic Vairochana, more frequently transliterated into Tibetan as Bairotsana. It would be too easy to identify this Berotsana with the 8th century Bairotsana who brought Dzogchen to Tibet. This disciple of Padmasambhava, however, belonged to another era and a different translation push and it is impossible that he saw these texts. We have no date on this translation but it is likely to have been very soon after Marpa's transmission of Mahamudra to Tibet.

The translations into English are based on the oral transmission of Khamtrul Rinpoche. In the years following that most fortunate teaching, I became increasingly absorbed by Dzogchen, and these seminal Mahamudra texts became marginalised. I focused on them again ten years later in London, in preparation for web publication, and revised some of them again in Kathmandu in 1995. In preparation for this publication I have thoroughly edited that work, abandoning some literal features of the Tibetan, reworking the translation to present the meaning in clearer English, sometimes leaving the literal translation behind at the expense of the subtleties of the Tibetan. Further, changes in basic English vocabulary, much influenced by Dzogchen, evolved over the years.

*An Addendum: The Life of Tilopa*
This secret biography of Tilopa, written mainly in prose, is included in this collection of poetry to demonstrate the 'secret' metaphoric language of the Bengali siddha tradition called *sandhyabhasa*. The text is couched in the form of a *namthar*, and appears to show development through time, but this is a cover for a metaphoric description of Tilopa's attainments − or singular attainment − of mahamudra-siddhi. This mahamudra-siddhi is both relative and ultimate, the relative being the attainment of the eight great siddhis and the ultimate, being buddha itself. This is the attainment accorded to the eighty-four mahasiddhas in their legends, although that series of life-stories are related in simple allegory while sandhyabhasa is employed only in the meditation instruction. Tilopa has only a minor place in Abhayadatta Sri's *Legends of the Mahasiddhas*, whereas this life-story, is not only the very earliest but it is also the most complete and rewarding.

*Acknowledgements*
My primary debt is to Khamtrul Rinpoche Dongyu Nyima for the gift of the text of the dohas and the oral transmission of Mahamudra. The Eighth Khamtrul Rinpoche of the Drukpa Kahgyu sub-school, was a scholar, an accomplished artist and a poet, besides an administrative genius responsible for the principal Drukpa Kahgyu establishment.

My rendering of the *Doha Treasury of Nakpopa* is based upon a translation made by Nicole Riggs (in Thailand in 2004), while the *Dohakosha of Maitripa* is her work with my slight editing. My thanks to her for her insight and generosity.

Regarding *The Life of Tilopa*, a number of Tibetan versions of this biography have come down to us, but all of them, as if determined to make the *sandhyabhasa* almost incomprehensible, are in poor grammatical Tibetan with various inconsistencies and anomalies. The translation published here is a thoroughly reworked version of the text published by Fabrizio Torricelli and Acharya Sangye T. Naga (*The Life of the Mahasiddha Tilopa*, Library of Tibetan Works and Archives, Dharamsala, 1995): my profound thanks to them. A very thorough scholastic analysis of the material available concerning the siddha Tilopa is published as a PhD thesis by Fabrizio Torricelli.

Keith Dowman
Tepoztlan
Mexico

January full moon 2020

## Saraha's Dohakosha
## The King's Song

Welcome to Arya Manjushri!
Welcome to the destroyer of demonic power!

The wind lashes calm water into rollers and breakers;
The King makes multifarious forms out of unity,
Seeing the many faces of Saraha, the Archer.

The cross-eyed fool sees one lamp as two:
The vision and the viewer are one,
You broken, brittle mind!

Many lamps are lit in the house,
But the blind are still in darkness:
*Sahaja* is all-pervasive
But the fool cannot see what is under his nose.

Just as many rivers are one in the ocean
Half-truths are swallowed by the one truth:
The sun's effulgence illuminates every dark corner.

Clouds draw water from the ocean to fall as rain
But moisture neither increases nor decreases:
Just so, *suchness* remains invariable, like the pure sky.

Replete with buddha-perfection
*Sahaja* is unitary, essential nature;
Beings are born into it and pass into it,
And neither being nor nonbeing can be.

Rejecting pure pleasure the fool roams abroad,
Hoping for mundane excitement;
Your mouth is full of honey now,
Swallow it while you can!

Fools try to avoid suffering,
The wise enact their pain.
Let others thirst after appearances
While we drink the cup of sky-nectar!

Flies eat filth, spurning sandalwood;
Lost to nirvana, you exacerbate confusion
Thirsting for the coarse and vulgar.

Rain water filling an ox's hoof-print
Evaporates under the hot sun;
Just so, imperfections of mind
All dissolve in perfect awareness.

Sea water absorbed by cloud turns sweet,
Just as the venom of passionate reaction
In a strong and selfless mind becomes elixir.

The unutterable is free of pain;
Nonmeditation gives true pleasure.
Though you fear the dragon's roar
The falling rain matures the crop.

Both beginning and end are here and now,
And the first is futile divorced from the last;
The rational fool imaging the inconceivable
Separates emptiness from compassion.

The bee instinctively knows
Where to find the cradle of honey;
How does the fool know
That samsara and nirvana are one?

Facing himself in a mirror
The fool sees an alien form;
The mind with truth forgotten
Serves untruth's outward sham.

A flower's fragrance intangible,
Still its scent pervades the air;

Just so, mandala circles are informed
By a formless presence.

Still water stung by an icy wind
Freezes hard in starched and jagged shapes;
In an emotional mind agitated by critical concepts
The unformed becomes hard and intractable.

Mind immaculate by nature is untouched
By any taint of samsara and nirvana;
Just as a jewel lost in a swamp
Retains its lustre but does not shine.

Pure awareness devolves into mental sloth,
And as sloth increases suffering grows;
Shoots sprout from the seed
And leaves from the shoot.

Separating unity from multiplicity in the mind
The light grows dim and you wander in lower realms;
Who is more deserving of pity than he
Who walks into fire with his eyes open?

Obsessed with sexual embrace
The fool imagines he knows ultimate truth,
Like someone who stands at the door
Flirting, gossiping about sex.

The wind stirs in the empty house
Exciting visions of pleasure;
Fallen out of celestial space, stung,
The yogin, tormented, faints away.

Like a brahmin taking rice and butter
Offering sacrifice to the flame,
Visualising substances as celestial ambrosia
He deludes himself that dream is ultimate reality.

Enlightening Brahma's seat in the fontanelle
Stroking the uvula in wanton delight,

Confused, believing binding pleasure to be spiritual release,
Some vain fools will call themselves yogins.

Believing that virtue is intrinsic awareness,
He mistakes the lock for the key;
Ignorant of the qualities of gem-stone
The fool calls green glass emerald.

His mind takes brass for gold,
Sensory pleasure for reality accomplished;
Clinging to the joy of ephemeral dream,
He calls his short-thrift life eternal bliss.

With a discursive understanding of the symbol EVAM
And the four mudras an analysis of each moment,
He labels his peak experience *sahaja*:
He is clinging to a reflection mistaken for the mirror.

Like befuddled deer leaping into a mirage of water,
Deluded fools in their ignorance cling to outer form,
And with their thirst unslaked, bound and confined,
They idealise their prison, pretending happiness.

The relatively real is now free of intellectual constructs,
And the ultimately real, active or quiescent, is no-mind;
This is the supreme, the highest of the high, immaculate:
Friends, know this sacred high!

In mind absorbed in concept-free *samadhi*,
Passion is immaculately pure;
Just as a lotus is rooted in the slime of a lake bottom,
So this sublime reality is embedded in polluted existence.

Make constant your vision of things as visionary dream
And you attain transcendence,
Instantaneous realisation and equanimity;
A strong mind binding dark demons,
Beyond thought, spontaneity is accomplished.

Appearances never shed their original radiance,
And formlessness never had a substantial nature;
A continuum of inimitable meditation
Inactive, stainless, is no-mind.

Thus 'I' is intellect, mind and mind-forms,
'I' the world, all seemingly alien show,
'I' the infinite variety of vision-viewer,
'I' the desire, the anger, the mental sloth —
And *bodhichitta*.

Here is a lamp lit in spiritual darkness
Healing the split riven by intellect
So that mental defilements are erased.
What is the nature of detachment?

Freedom cannot be denied nor yet affirmed,
And ungraspable it is inconceivable.
Through concepts fools are bound,
While concept-free immaculate *sahaja* rules.

Concepts of unity and diversity are impotent;
Awareness alone brings freedom to sentient beings.
Cognition of radiance is strong meditation:
Abide in a calm, quiescent mind.

Reaching the joy-swollen land
The power of seeing expands
With delight and laughter
And without separation in the chase.

From joy, buds of pure pleasure emerge,
Bursting into blossom of highest pleasure,
And so long as outflows are contained
Unutterable delight will surely mature.

What, where and by whom are naught,
Yet the entire event is crucial;

Whether love and attachment or desirelessness
The nature of cognition is emptiness.

Like pigs we wallow in this sensory mire
But what can stain our pearly mind?
Nothing whatsoever can infect us,
And by nothing can we ever be bound.

*This cache of aphorisms (doha mdzod), songs of existential freedom (spyod pa'i glu, charyagiti) was composed by the glorious master-yogin Saraha.*

## Saraha's Dohakosha:
## Mahamudra Pith Precepts
## The Queen Doha

Welcome to Glorious Vajra Dakini!
Welcome to the pure delight of perfect awareness!

*This treasury of verses is divided into three parts:*
*I. The Natural State of Mahamudra;*
*II Mahamudra as the Way;*
*III The Consummation of Mahamudra.*[1]

*The sub-divisions of these parts consist of dohas gathered under common heads.*

### I. Mahamudra as the Natural State

*1. What is Mahamudra?*

Movement or stillness, pulsation or rest,
All existence is appearance and emptiness,
And all things whatsoever have a sky-like nature
That can never be lost in time or space.
That is Mahamudra.

This sky-like nature cannot be shown:
It is beyond existence and non-existence,
Beyond assertion, negation and all ontology,
Beyond verbal power and metaphor to convey.

But 'sky', 'mind' and 'things-in-themselves',
These three distinct names are nominal caprice,
Meaningless deceptive labels.

All seeming elements of reality[2] are mind,
For other than mind not an atom exists;
Whoever realises original no-mind
Gains the realisation of timeless buddha.

The ten thousand things are conventional names,
No sensory element more than mere label.
Essential nature arisen out of nothing,
Unrevealed, indemonstrable,
How can that inscrutable nature be known?
Only a fool asserts substantial self-nature,
But then who can confidently deny it?

If mind exists absolutely then all things must be substantial;
And if mind is nonexistent, how can anything be known?
Explore the appearances of mind and sensory elements
And nothing is discovered.

Then seeking the seeker, again nothing:
In time nothing substantial arises or ceases to be
And whatever arises never changes,
And its nature is pure delight.

All appearances are *dharmakaya*,
All sentient beings are buddha,
All volition and action are forever *dharmadhatu*,[3]
And all mental constructs are rabbits' horns.

*2. Showing that failing to intuit suchness we are deluded.*

Ayah! This wheel of life!
The light of the unclouded sun is all-embracing,
But the eyeless live in perpetual darkness;
The innate absolute is everywhere,
But deluded fools are blind!

In our failure to intuit no-mind
Our fantasies occlude mind's true nature.
Like a madman who plays with evil spirits
We pile futile suffering upon our head;
Playing with the ogres of reification[4] and dualization,
We provoke so much meaningless pain.

Some of us tie ourselves to nit-picking argument;
Ignoring the presence within, we seek it outside;

Clutching at hallucination and mirage
We ravage the foliage, ignoring the root,
All blind to the snare of our every move.

*3. Showing the nature of the Mountain Recluse's insight.*

KYE HO! Listen to this!
Never moving out of reality
Yet you children are blind!

When I perceived my beginning and my end
I saw my self and was left with my self alone.
Looking into this solitary self, no self could I find;
There was nothing to see and no-one to see it,
So nothing can be said of it. How can it possibly be grasped?
At that time I was purified in original mind
And the mountain recluse gained his realisation.

The lioness's dugs are not for everyone.
When her roar startles the jungle
Her hungry cubs run to her
While lesser creatures tremble in fear.
When primordial pure delight is taught
The foolish, opinionated, become contentious,
But the hair of the elect bristles with joy.

*IIa. Mahamudra as the Way: Cutting Through by Seeing*

*1. Showing the manner of seeing.*

KYE HO! Now listen to this!
Look at ourselves with unwavering focus
And we can intuit our own *suchness*.
Even distractions then appear as Mahamudra,
And every moment, every specific, reflexively released,
Dissolves into the sphere of pure delight.

Dreaming dreams, good and bad, awaking,
Both equally are known to be dream.

After all our hopes and fears have fallen away
Who then is attached to his dreams?

Samsara or nirvana, penetrated to the core,
Every moment is known equally as insubstantial.
Thoughts touched by hope or fear abandoned,
Why then strive to reject this or cultivate that?

All appearance, all sound, is like magical illusion,
Hallucination, reflection or echo
And no discrete or concrete entities exist.
The conjurer is the sky-like nature of mind.
Who can grasp a space without centre or boundary?

Just as both Ganga and Jumna
Taste salty in the saline ocean,
The welter of imaginings and every mental event
Taste alike in the field of the *dharmadhatu*.

*2. Showing the way to realisation.*

Searching spaciousness
Without centre or circumference
Nothing can be seen;
Exploring the mind and experience,
Finding no trace of anything solid,
Failing to find the mind that is exploring,
Seeing nothing, *that* is truly seeing.

*3. The way to attain unchangeable realisation.*

Like a crow caught on a ship at sea,
Flying off, circling, returning to the mast,
The aspiring mind, its dualization arrested,
Settles in the pristine nature of its original face.
Unmoved by any contingency,
Lurking hopes and fears destroyed,
That is diamond-mind, Vajrasattva.

## IIb. Mahamudra as the Way: Meditation

### 1. Demonstrating Mahamudra nonmeditation

The mind in itself, thoroughly explored, is like the sky;
Nonmeditation arrests the dualizing function of mind
And genuine natural perception in the common light of day
Is untarnished by alluring fictions –
The mind inherently pure can never be defiled.
Without grasping or releasing mind-forms, rest easy.

No meditative process exists in unrealised mind
And neither meditator nor object arises in realised mind,
Sky as sky can never be objectified.
Likewise, emptiness cannot meditate on emptiness;
The unity of metamorphic, multiform perception,
Like a mixture of milk and water,
Arises constantly in the one taste of pure delight.

### ii. Showing meditation as indistinguishable from nonmeditation.

In that way, in all situations and at all times,
Blend with the authentic, unlimited mental sphere of inaction:
Sustaining *suchness* is conventional Mahamudra meditation.

The wind blows where it lists and the mind is not bound:
Let unstructured perception wander like a small child.
When reflective thought arises, look at its empty nature,
Remembering that waves are not different from water.

### iii. Showing by simile that free of its reifying tendencies, released from the three cogs (subject, object, interaction), ordinary consciousness is Mahamudra as the Way.

In unstructured, nonconceptual Mahamudra,
Lacking any hint of technique, nonmeditation arises;
In actual nonmeditation, only supreme meditation.

The taste of pure delight is coincident with nonduality,
The one flavour of two drops of water commingling.
In this sphere of the sameness of nonmeditation
Allowing its mental projections, the mind is perfectly serene.

## IIc. Meditation as the Way: Activity

*1. Showing the equivocal praxis of Mahamudra.*

KYE HO! Listen to this with joy!
In the yoga of ultimate nonduality
Why would I reject or cultivate anything?
I have left attachment and antipathy behind,
But do not call me a child.
Like the equivocal philosopher's stone
The yogin's behaviour is uncertain.
But he takes unwarranted criticism of his equivocation
For the yogin's mind is always one,
Although in singularity it still has no substantiality,
And his multifarious enactments are baseless.
Free and unpredictable, like a madman,
His uninhibited behaviour seems like the play of a child.

*2. Showing that in his enactment he is immune to external circumstances.*

EHMA HO! Listen with joy!
The yogin's lotus-like mind, immune to evil,
Thrives in the slime of existence.
Contented, hunger assuaged and thirst slaked,
Or diseased in body and stricken in mind,
Enacting any of innumerable dramas,
He is never trapped, never freed,
And always innocent.

*3. Showing how the yogin's detached compassion arises spontaneously to benefit others.*

The pain and exhaustion of benighted beings arising
In the realised yogin's dispassionate sphere,
By dint of unrestrained compassion his tears flow,
And in the epitome of charity, self and others are reconciled.

With resolution in emptiness, freed of desire, anger and sloth,
All enactment is unreal like the figment of dream;

With free-flowing love, joyful and guileless,
The buddha-magician casts his healing spell.

*III. Mahamudra as Consummation*

*1. Showing the certainty of goal-attainment.*

Our sky-like nature, pure from the beginning,
Neither lost nor gained,.
Unstructured, nonconceptual Mahamudra,
Mahamudra the goal, cannot be lost.
Hope itself is originally unborn,
So how can anything go missing or be gotten?
If anything is to be acquired by anyone
What meaning have the four precepts?[5]

*2. Showing the error in trying to attain what is already in hand.*

Like deluded deer leaping towards a mirage of water,
Poor fools tormented by unnameable desire
Strive constantly to satisfy insatiable longing,
Never getting near their goal.

*3. Attainment of nothing whatsoever itself is understood as the accomplishment of Vajradhara.*

A mirage of water on a dry plain
Gives the illusion of water where there is none;
Just so, the originally pure analytic mind
Provides neither temporal nor ultimate truth.

Like a wish-fulfilling gem or a wish-granting tree,
The power of aspiration fulfils all hopes.
And remember that all propositions about the external world,
All are vanity, mere convention,
And nothing whatsoever is absolute.

*Colophon*
*That is the* Dohakosha of Mahamudra Precepts *(in Sanskrit:* Dohakosha nama mahamudra upadesha*; in Tibetan:* Doha mdzod zhes bya ba mahamudra man ngag), *composed by the Mountain Recluse Saraha. It was translated into the Tibetan language by the Indian Sage Vairochana Rakshita.*

## Endnotes to Saraha's Queen's Song

[1] The divisions of the text in the original are unaccountable. The present divisions are the most logical that could be devised.

[2] The word 'reality' appears nowhere in the text. Whatever word Saraha used in Buddhist Sanskrit, the Tibetan translator found it necessary to use a word that would not allow an opponent to accuse him of incipient Brahmanism – belief in an atman or soul. The word *de nyid* or its synonyms – which has been translated as 'reality' when unavoidable – is literally 'itself', or 'thatness', or '*suchness'*.

[3] The technical expressions *chos sku* and *chos dbyings*, have been translated *dharmakaya* and *dharmadhatu* herein.

[4] 'Reification' is shorthand for 'belief in the substantiality of external objects derived from the mental processes that project seemingly concrete appearances'.

[5] The four Mahamudra SAMAYAS: Non-abandonment of obscuration; non-application of any remedy; nonmeditation upon *tathata*; non-aspiration or anticipation (from Shang Rinpoche).

# A Charyagiti of Saraha

1. Our own concepts and projects create samsara and nirvana;
   By our own minds are we imprisoned in this world.

2. I am a stupid yogin with a thought-free mind;
   What is birth and death to me?

3. Birth is just like death, an empty dream,
   And the living and the dead are the same.

4. Whoever here is afraid of birth and dying,
   He tries to produce gold out of mercury.

5. The pilgrim who roams the earth or his own mind
   How can he avoid old age and dying?

6. Which comes first, spontaneity or buddha-karma?
   Saraha says, 'My religion is a thought-free mind.'

### *Line by Line Commentary*

1. The basic proclivity of a mind lacking awareness of the original state of things is to create a dualistic universe in which 'I' and 'it' are separate entities, where mental concepts label and define, and emotional projections distort every perception. Accordingly one is bound by the mind and only by the mind can one be released from existence.

2. Here Saraha asserts his enlightened state of mind by self-deprecation and the implication that he identifies with the empty strata of being in which creation and cessation are events of equal temporal insignificance, yet both pure pleasure.

3. Since nothing is to be created, all things being free of a self, an *ens*, or any substantial principle, phenomena are 'unoriginated' or

'unborn'; they also therefore have no cessation. Further, 'no distinction between dream and the awakened state can arise'.

4. The Tibetan translation of the original Apabhramsa appears to be incorrect. This would be preferable:

> Whoever here has no fear of birth and dying,
> He transforms mercury into gold.

The alchemical metaphor of transforming mercury into gold is valid on every level of yoga, including the supreme (*anuttara*) level where immortality has the most meaning, and the siddhas of Saraha's Mahamudra lineage would have been initiates of the *rasayana* tantra. However, as the Apabhramsa is ambiguous and Munidatta, the commentator, favours the interpretation of the alchemical yogin performing a mundane sadhana for a temporal end, the mood in Saraha's song and Munidatta's commentary has been preferred.

5. The 'childish' yogin with an active disposition is a pilgrim who travels from powerplace to powerplace in India, while the inactive yogin practices mantra and takes drugs and arrives in the paradise of the gods.

6. 'Is karma due to birth or birth due to karma?' Munidatta interprets birth as the generation of a powerful state of yoga free of an actor or of an action and the karma associated with this state is necessarily non-karma, non-action, which is Mahamudra motivation. Saraha is asking which came first, the yogin's samadhi or his perfect action. His answer, according to Munidatta: 'Since the yogin's absolute knowledge and awareness is non-referential and thought-free, it is all the same.'

## Nakpopa's Dohakosha

This way to the natural state! Welcome!

*This text has two parts: first, On the cessation of extreme beliefs of view, meditation, action and result; and, second, On unfathomable, unrestricted suchness.*

*1. On the Cessation of Extreme Views, Meditation, Action and Result*

*(i) On the cessation of extreme views*
Proud worldly people, with your texts and logic,
Claim, 'I know emptiness.' But they're wrong.

Understanding is impossible and there's no way 'in' –
Emptiness is empty of emptiness too.

No birth can exist, because of birthlessness,
No stuffing in dying, becoming or rebirth.

The intellect conceives concepts not realisation;
The problem can never be resolved intellectually.

*(ii) On the cessation of extreme meditation*
Conceptual thought is delusive thought,
Neither the thinker nor the thought is truly existent.
Contingent truth, ephemeral truth,
Paves the path of delusion.

When the intellect finds its way home,
Home to the mighty experience of samadhi,
It finds knowledge of the *sugatas*,
And the wrathful deities and their retinues.

*(iii) On the cessation of extreme action*
It would be a mistake to make any effort here!
Giving and taking are both so tiresome!

*(iv) On the cessation of extreme result*
The *dharmakaya* is like the sky –
Reaching for it is like a blind beggar stretching for alms;
Hoping for it is like a deer's expectation in chasing a mirage.
Already and ever buddha,
What a blunder to seek it!

*2. On unfathomable, unrestricted suchness*

Fantasy-beings enter the middle way,
Where dream-forests crown sky-mountains,
Dream-elephants march to a mirage-oasis,
And the sons of barren women
Rule the gandharva cloud-kingdom.

I, Nakpopa, don't want change.
I don't 'walk a path'. I stay natural.
Realising *suchness,* I don't appraise it.

Knowing definitive truth without critique,
Grip on the emptiness/appearance dualism slips away
And phenomena no longer impinging, the intellect surrenders.

*This completes the* Dohakosha of Nakpopa *(in Sanskrit:* Doha kosha nama; *in Tibetan:* Doha mdzod). *Translated into Tibetan by Berotsana.*

# Tilopa's Mahamudra Instruction to Naropa in Twenty-eight Vajra-Verses: The Gangama

A humble welcome to the Eighty-four Mahasiddhas, to
Mahamudra, to Vajra Dakini!

Mahamudra cannot be taught. But most intelligent Naropa,
You have undergone rigorous austerity,
With forbearance in suffering and devotion to the Guru,
So most fortunate yogin, take this pith instruction to heart.

Where is space supported? Upon what does it rest?
Like space, Mahamudra is dependent upon nothing.
Relax and settle in the continuum of unalloyed purity,
And, your shackles loosening, freedom is certain.

Gazing intently into the empty sky, vision ceases;
Likewise, when mind gazes into mind itself,
The train of discursive and conceptual thought ends
And we gain enlightenment.

Like the morning mist dissolving,
Going nowhere, simply ceasing,
Incessant conceptualisation ends
When we see our mind's true nature.

Spaciousness has neither colour nor shape
And it cannot become black or white;
Like that, mind's essence is beyond colour and shape
And it cannot be spoiled by black or white deeds.

The darkness of a thousand aeons is unable
To dim the crystal clarity of the sun's core;
Likewise, aeons of samsara have no power
To veil the clear light of the mind.

Although space has been designated 'empty',
In truth it is beyond description;
The nature of mind is 'clear light',
But every ascription is verbal fiction.

The mind's original nature is spaciousness;
It pervades and embraces all things under the sun.

Be still, stay relaxed in genuine ease,
Be quiet, let sound reverberate as echo,
Keep the mind silent, watch the ending of all worlds.

The body is empty like the stem of a reed
And the mind, like space, transcends thought:
Relax into intrinsic nature with neither abandon nor control –
Mind without object is Mahamudra –
And, with practice perfected, enlightenment arises.

Mahamudra's clear light is not revealed
Through canonical scriptures or metaphysical treatises,
In the mantravada, the paramitas or the tripitaka:
The clear light is veiled by concepts and ideals.

Harbouring rigid precepts the true samaya is impaired,
But with cessation of mental activity all fixed notions subside;
When the swell of the ocean is at one with its peaceful depths,
When mind never strays from indeterminate, nonconceptual truth,
The unbroken samaya is a lamp lit in spiritual darkness.

Free of intellectual conceits, disavowing dogmatic principles,
The truth of every school and scripture is revealed.

Absorbed in Mahamudra, we are free from the samsaric prison;
Poised in Mahamudra, guilt and negativity are consumed;
As masters of Mahamudra we light the way.
The ignorant fool disdaining Mahamudra
Struggles in the flood of samsara.
Pity those who suffer constant anxiety!

Sick of unrelenting pain, desiring release, serve a master,
For when he touches our heart, our mind is liberated.


KYE HO! Listen with joy!
Investing in samsara is futile – it causes anxiety.
Erudite involvement is pointless – seek only truth itself.

In transcendence of mind's dualities lies true vision;
In a still and silent mind is true meditation;
Spontaneity allows true activity;
All hopes and fears abandoned, the goal is attained.

Beyond mental images the mind is clear:
Following no path we tread the buddha-path;
And employing no technique enlightenment reigns.

KYE MA! Listen with sympathy!
With insight into our sorry everyday predicament,
Realising that nothing can last, that all is dreamlike illusion,
Meaningless illusion, provoking frustration and boredom,
Turn around and abandon selfish pursuits.

Severing involvement with our homeland and friends
And meditating alone in a forest or mountain retreat,
Staying there in nonmeditation,
Attaining no-attainment, we attain Mahamudra.

A tree spreads its branches and sprouts leaves,
But cut its root and its foliage withers;
When the root of the mind is severed,
The branches of samsara die.

A single lamp dispels a thousand aeons' darkness;
A single flash of the mind's clear light
Erases ages of karmic conditioning and blindness.

KYE HO! Listen with joy!
The truth beyond mind cannot be grasped by mind
And nonaction is lost in compulsive activity.
To realise the meaning of nonaction and beyond mind,
Cut the mind at its root and rest in naked awareness.

Allow the muddy waters of mental activity to settle;
Restraining both positive and negative projections leave
      appearances alone,
For the phenomenal world without addition or subtraction is
      Mahamudra.

The unborn omnipresent ground dissolves impulsions and
      delusions:
Do not be conceited or calculating – rest in the unborn essence
And let all concepts of self and other melt away.

The highest vision opens every gate,
The highest meditation plumbs infinite depths,
The highest activity is ungoverned yet decisive
And the highest goal is ordinary being devoid of hope and fear.

At first our karma is like a river falling through a gorge;
In mid-course it flows like a meandering river Ganga;
And finally, as it runs into the ocean,
Consummation, like the meeting of mother and son.

If mind is dull and these instructions are beyond us,
Then retain essential breath and expel the sap of awareness,
Practise fixed gazes, methods of focussing the mind,
Disciplining ourselves until awareness rules.

Connecting with a *karmamudra*
Awareness of pure pleasure and emptiness may arise:
In a union of perfect insight and skilful means
Send down, retain and then draw up *bodhichitta*,
And retracting it to its source, saturate the entire body.
But only if attachment is absent will pure awareness arise.

Thus gaining long-life and eternal youth, waxing like the moon,
Radiant and clear, with the strength of a lion,
We attain mundane power and enlightenment.

May these Mahamudra pith precepts,
Remain in the hearts of fortunate beings.

*Colophon*
Tilopa's Mahamudra Instruction to Naropa in Twenty-eight Vajra-Verses (*in Tibetan*: Phyag rgya chen po'i man ngag: Phyag rgya chen po rdo rje'i tsig rkang nyi shu rtsa brgyad pa) *was transmitted by the Great Guru and Mahasiddha Tilopa to the Kashmiri pandit, sage and siddha, Naropa, near the banks of the river Ganga upon the completion of his twelve austerities. Naropa taught the teaching in Sanskrit in the form of twenty-eight verses to the great Tibetan translator Marpa Chokyi Lodro, who made a free translation of it at his village of Pulahari on the Tibet-Bhutan borde*

# Tilopa's Dohakosha

Welcome to Glorious Vajrasattva!
Welcome to Mahamudra!
Welcome to the unchanging intrinsic nature of cognition!

*The Complete Teaching*

*View*
The body-mind, the elements of perception, the sense-fields,
All appear as Mahamudra and dissolve into Mahamudra:
Only Mahamudra exists!

Temporal relativity and its absence are concept-free,
For meaning and value are no longer projected.

All appearance is illusory, but in its self-nature
Neither beginning nor end, nor first nor last.

Whatever enters the intellectual sphere
Loses its authenticity in dualization –
Both guru and disciple demote the intellect.

Without differentiating mind from no-mind,
Focus upon the unity that thaws multiplicity.
Clinging to unity, however, pure value is somniferous.

*Meditation*
I, Tilopa, have nothing to teach.
My existence is solitary but I am never alone.
My eyes are closed but I do not sleep.
My mind is innocent but I am free of duplicity.

Know the stream of primal purity in a silent mind
And in nonverbal, unqualified *suchness*,
Apprehend fortuitous forms of awareness.

We may sense delusiveness, but do not discriminate.
What then is satisfaction and frustration, success and failure?

*Action*
Do not copy the ascetic enduring austerity in the forest,
We will not find happiness in cleanliness and ritual purity
And we will not find freedom in worship of the gods:
Discover indiscriminate mind in the contingencies of the path.

*The Goal*
*The Circumstantial Goal*
The goal is total awareness, the intrinsic nature of cognition.
On the path of spontaneous insight, clinging to nothing,
Security and ambition renounced, hope and fear forgotten,
Supports and defences discarded, we may be content.

*The Ultimate Goal*
The mind's self-interest assuaged, ego disbands,
And the dichotomies of the waking-dream are resolved.


*The Epitome*

Without thought, deliberation or analysis,
Without meditation or action,
Without doubt or expectation,
Mental constructs – all dualities
Spontaneously disperse
And the original face of mind shines through.


*Colophon*
*Tilopa's Dohakosha, his final statement upon the practice of Mahamudra, was translated from Sanskrit into Tibetan by the Indian Sage Berotsana.*

## Naropa's Concise Mahamudra View

Welcome to Vajra Varahi!
Welcome to the Omniscient Protector, Lord of Beings!

Following both scripture and oral tradition
I have written this final summation.

Our experience of phenomena
Rests in intrinsic awareness.
Appearances are clear and luminous
Purely a function of awareness.
Without the nature of mind
There can be no contact and experience.
That is self-evident truth:
'All things exist in the mind'.

The ground of all things, the mind in itself,
Self-examined, explored by awareness,
Knows only the clear light of its nature.
Is this clear light the same or different
From adventitious tainting thoughts?
The sages have examined this tantalising question,
And after much discussion this is the definitive answer:

Emptiness itself is the mind's awareness.
It is *bodhichitta* – enlightened mind!
It is buddha-potential!
It is the matrix of the buddha-sugatas!
Savouring the taste of every experience
It is pure pleasure, *mahasukha*!
It is consciousness of mantra as sound!
It is skilful means and perfect insight!
It is vastness and depth!
It is Samantabhadra/Samantabhadri!

Ultimate buddha-perception functions here
As pure awareness of the field of empty light-form
And even tainted intrinsic awareness,
That itself is self-sprung pure awareness.
It is awareness and therefore it is clarity.

As intrinsic awareness it is thought-free,
For thought disperses in intrinsic awareness,
And since concepts likewise disperse,
Mind is concept-free.
In its clarity thought-free pure awareness,
That is *sugata* pure-awareness.

In the clear light of its own nature
The mind is pure awareness:
'Do not seek buddha elsewhere!'

When the mind is emotionally toned
By the adventitious emergence of conceptual thought,
When it devolves into pure or impure states,
Like water, gold or space,
The clear light of its nature is free
Of even a hair's tip of anything concrete.

Consider the treasure house of the sky:
Its existence cannot be established
But it cannot in the least be disproven;
Now seemingly real, now as unreal,
It cannot be established as either,
And it cannot be both —
It is not a discrete entity.

It is not neither this nor that
And nor can it be both.
There can be no living beings
And nor are there no living beings.
Free of every verbal construction,
This is the ultimate truth —
'The mind's nature is spaciousness.'

This intrinsic awareness beyond verbal construction
In its emptiness is form and in its form emptiness;
Form and emptiness are one,
Just like water and the moon's reflection.
This is nonduality –
'Spaciousness has no ground.'

This intrinsic awareness beyond verbal construction,
That is the ground of samsara!
It is nirvana!
It is the transcendent middle way!
It is what is to be 'seen' – the vision!
It is the focus of nonmeditation!
It is the goal!
It is undeniable logical truth!

It is known in its temporal aspect
As the thread of motivation, technique and objective,
As ground, path and goal.
It is known as the contents of consciousness,
As the constituents of samsara,
And as the integrated field of phenomena.


EHMA HO!
The six kinds of living beings, gods and demons,
All forms of the mind's defilement,
Emanate in the boundless fields of space
As conceptual or illusory phenomena – nirvana.

Such intrinsic awareness beyond construction,
Free of conceptual defilement,
That is non-abiding absolute nirvana!
It is Vajrasattva!
It is the Sixth Buddha!
It is the Sixth Buddha Family!
It is Manjushrikumara!
It is Vairochana!
It is the *dharmakaya* and pure pleasure!
It is unity of polarity, *yuganaddha*!

It is the fourth empowerment!
It is innate joy, s*ahajananda*!
It is inherent purity!

Such innumerable expressions
Taken from sutra and tantra and used here,
All are employed in the oral tradition.

EHMA HO!
The immaculate fields of space
Filled with magical illusory emanation,
And mind's stainless nature,
Comprise the buddha-body of form.

Mandalas of apparitional form,
Marvellous illusory emanation,
Fill the wide sky.

Heretical outsiders,
Believing in a soul, an ego, a controller,
Minds tainted by emotional prejudice,
Lose themselves in philosophical speculation.

Even the Listeners, Hermits
And Mind Only sages of our own school
Conceive subject and object as things apart,
Separate from nondual, ultimate, perfection.
Holding delusion and truth as two
They are entangled in a conceptual web.

But through our sure vision,
Meditation and action in perfect harmony,
Purity and clarity – enlightenment – is inborn.
That is the winner.

If view does not correspond to *suchness*
And meditation and action are perverse,
The pain of separation is inevitable –
A blind man without a guide!

Reality, deep and vast as the ocean,
My mind like a frog in a well –
How can I plumb the murky depths?
The wise man repentant must be patient.

Through the merit accrued herein
May the fortunate fearless being
Rid himself of defiling delusion
And generate perfect insight.

*This concludes* Lord Naropa's Concise Mahamudra View *(in Sanskrit: Adhi siddhi sama nama;* in Tibetan*: Lta ba mdor bsdus). The translator Marpa Chokyi Lodro, having heard it from the Pandita Jnana Siddhi (Yeshe Drupa) himself, translated it into Tibetan.*

# Virupa's Dohakosha

Glorious Vajrasattva: welcome to you!
Victorious, virtuous, transcendent Nairatma: welcome!

*The text has three sections:*
*I. Absolute-Truth Mahamudra: The Basic Natural Condition*
*II. Relative-Truth Mahamudra: How to Tread the Path.*
*III. The Inseparability of these Two Truths*

*I. Absolute-Truth Mahamudra: The Basic Natural Condition*

EMA HO!
Mahamudra is the sameness of samsara and nirvana.
Because it knows no origin, it is as pure as the sky;
Because it is free of identity, it is signless;
Because it is formless, it has no manifestation.
It cannot be examined or analysed;
It cannot be exemplified:
Yet it is not defined by non-example:
It transcends intellectual expression.

Mahamudra does not last, yet it has no end;
It is not samsara, yet not nirvana;
It is no appearance, yet not emptiness;
It has no substance, yet not insubstantial.
It is not 'the unborn' nor 'the natural state';
It is not 'what transcends the intellect';
It is not existent, yet not nonexistent.

Because no verbal definition holds,
It cannot be defined in dualistic terms:
It is original sameness.

Much is said of its essence, its true meaning, and its function:
But then, what of the rabbit's horns?
Much can be said of their sharpness or dullness!

No thing exists but in the imagination,
For objective appearance is without any substance.
All is mere name, mere frame, pure imputation.
And name and meaning are the same.

Mahamudra is primary and co-emergent – unsought.
Mahamudra is of mind, a name and an emptiness –
    spaciousness.
Mahamudra is unborn quintessence – no thing with a label,
Like space, all-pervading, imperishable – unchanging,
Ubiquitous emptiness, without any self-nature.

Without character,
It cannot be remembered or thought of:
It has no identity.
It cannot bind or fetter:
Never leaving its interior natural state.

Sentient life is Mahamudra emanation,
Primordially birthless – a constant reality-expanse.
The dualities of happiness and sadness et al,
The play of Mahamudra is reality laid bare.
Without any essence, a flickering display,
It never loses the seal of natural-state emptiness.

## II. Relative-Truth Mahamudra: How to Tread the Path.

### 1. The Deluded Way to Tread the Path

Some lamas grant empowerment but cause distress;
Some declaim HUNG and PHAT and count their beads;
Some consume dung and urine, blood, semen and flesh;
Some rest in the illusions of energy channels and flows.

### 2. A Non-Deluded Way to Tread the Path

*(i) Instruction on the Definitive View*
*(ii) Instruction on Meditation*
*iii) Instruction on Action: Treading the Path*
*(iv) Instruction on the Goal: The Perfection of Mahamudra*

*(i) Oral Instruction on the Definitive View*

EMA HO!
Anchored by the lama, cognise nonunderstanding!
Delusion is every single thing – nonrealisation!
Nothing is to be realised, no one to realise,
No absence of realisation is possible.
Neither freedom nor constraint existing
Only a natural constancy abides.
With this definitive view all is fulfilment.

Variegated form all shines as suchness
And accepting and rejecting mind do not arise.
Meditation and no-meditation are identical,
And pejorative distinctions do not cause moral pollution.
No basis for dualizing objectivity can arise.

Without concepts of deed and doer,
Thought is free of concrete reference points.
Without projections larded with hope or fear,
Attachment becomes thoroughly inverted.

With realisation of the lama's natural state,
Mental activity dissolves fast in the reality-sphere.
In the stream of consciousness, empty of attachment,
Uncontrived phenomena freely rise and fall.

Unbound, but without pride or emotional flaws,
Respectful, supported by like-minds,
Free of thought-streams, without doubt,
Knowledge and knowing are emptied,
And reality itself resumes.

Ignorant of this innate Mahamudra,
Incessant duality-fed longing will endure,
Obfuscating thought will persist,
The unerring truth will be hidden,

And we drift or we spin in samsara.
Hungry, craving fame and gain, on a graduated path,
Practicing the dharma, and gaining some insight,
Achieving blessings, boons and powers,
That is all illusion – pay it no heed.

If we try to objectify and hold on to *suchness*,
We will suffer and fall, spiralling through samsara.
Focus on the ground of things, at the essence of mind –
And seeing nothing, the mind disengaged, we are free.

*(ii) Oral Instructions on Meditative Experience*

In the field of mind's pure nature,
No assertion of *suchness* as this or that can arise;
Free of meditation and object of meditation,
Rest detached without assertion or negation.

We may conceive of emptiness, birthlessness, the transcendental,
We may identify with the beyond and much else besides,
But that is not is our natural condition – far from it!
Rest in ease, without notions of emptiness or non-emptiness.

Let go, beyond resting and non-resting,
Like a zombie, without dualistic impulsion.

Aware of the reality-state, abiding there,
Dualistic tendencies will quickly disperse;
Distracted – mesmerised – by conceptual thought,
Realisation lost, dualistic tendencies persist.

When eyesight fails, for example,
An eye disease is indicated;
When eyesight is bright,
No need for the optician.

When we think we have found the natural state,
We have merely become attached to holistic experience;

When we attach reference points to the true meaning,
Our meditation has led us astray.

*(iii) Oral Instruction on Action: Treading the Path*
*This is divided into three parts: first, the actual practice; second, the wrong practice; and third, the Mahamudra samaya.*

*a) The Actual Practice*

Be aware that attachment to pleasure
Initiates craving and addiction;
But hardship is desirable,
Engendering clarity in the yogi.

Do not reject negative states –
Recognise their value and attend.
In adversity lies fulfilment,
Just as the whipped horse is encouraged.

Whoever has understanding and realisation,
But no practical experience,
He has the problem
Of excellent eyesight but no real spine.

Act out the meaning unglued from determinacy,
Without denial or assertion, without method or goal,
Without means or end,
Let spontaneity arise in the moment!

*b) The Wrong Practice*

Overwhelmed by attachment and craving,
We may reject everything – or pursue everything.
In neither case is that tantra-yoga:
It is wrong practice.

*c) The Mahamudra Samaya*

We may have conviction that we are buddha,
And still we accumulate optimal merit.

We are bold and fearless in samsara,
And we still avoid the slightest negative act.

We perceive all phenomena as empty,
Boundless and as limpid as the sky,
And we resist all preferences and partialities.

We reach the end of dualistic possibility,
And lacking anything to hold on to, we do not boast.

We realise that self and other are nondual,
And we aspire to benefit beings.

Our conviction is strong, a guide redundant,
And still we keep the kind lama above our head.

*(iv) Oral Instruction on the Outcome – the Perfection of Mahamudra – can be divided into temporary and ultimate.*

*a) Result in the Moment*

No one to see and nothing to be seen! – such distinctions fall away.
Practitioner and practice dissolve! – no effort or success.
No goal to attain! – hopes and fears disperse.
No self to uproot! – demons are defeated.
No belief in a reality! – no samsara, no nirvana.

*b) Timeless Result*

Awareness pure in its own ground:
> that is 'perfect enlightenment'.
Phenomena and intellect consumed:
> that is 'nirvana'.
No contrivance, no change:
> that is release from all bias.

*c) The Inseparability of the Two Truths*

EMA HO!
However we know, it is 'great Mahamudra
Or is it 'emptiness'? – grand words, but just words.

Instant after instant, all empty of essence,
And what self is there to realise it?
No one at all!
Thus 'buddha' is only a word, without import,
An expression for devotees and academics.

A magical show, an empty display,
'Mahamudra' is a word for unripe minds.
'Deluded' and 'undeluded' are empty words,
For who is present to experience delusion?
Nirvana? the result? not so much as a trace,
For who is present to make objective search?
Likewise 'freedom' and 'bondage' are both delusory.

Any path to liberation is redundant:
Quiet space and pure realm are fantasy,
'Momentary' and 'timeless' are logical labels,
And in reality-expanse, no two truths and no reality.

*This doha (in Sanskrit: Doha kosha nama; in Tibetan: Doha mdzod) was composed by the great yogi Virupa. It was translated into Tibetan by the Indian master Berotsana.*

## Maitripa's Essential Mahamudra Verses

Humble welcome to innermost bliss!

Were I to explain Mahamudra, I would say –
All phenomena? Our own mind!
Looking outside for meaning, we get confused;
Phenomena are like dream, all empty of true nature,

And the mind that is the flux of awareness:
No self-nature: just energy-flow,
No true nature: just like the sky,
All phenomena are alike, sky-like.

That's what we call Mahamudra:
It doesn't have any identity to show
And for that reason, the nature of mind
Is itself that very Mahamudra
(Which is uncompounded and cannot change).

Realising the *suchness* of things, we recognise
All that comes up, all that goes on, as Mahamudra,
The all-pervasive *dharmakaya*.

Rest in true nature, free of fabrication,
Meditate without searching for *dharmakaya* –
Dharmakaya cannot be thought.
If our mind searches, our meditation is confounded.

Because Mahamudra is spaciousness
And like magical show,
Neither meditation nor nonmeditation,
How can we be separate from it? or inseparable?
That's how the yogin sees it!

Then aware of the *suchness* of all good and bad
We are liberated.

Neurotic emotions are great awareness,
To yogins as trees are to fire – fuel!

What are notions of going or staying?
Or, for that matter, 'meditating' in solitude?
If we don't see this,
We can only be superficially free.

But if we do get it, what can ever bind us?
We abide constantly in an undistracted state.
Trying to adjust body and mind won't produce meditation.
Trying to apply technique won't produce meditation either.

Look! nothing can be ultimately established,
Whatever appears has no intrinsic nature.
Appearances perceived: *suchness*, self-liberated.
Thought that perceives: spacious awareness, self-liberated.
Non-duality, sameness of perceiver and perceived: the
    *dharmakaya*.

Like a wide stream endlessly flowing,
Whatever its phase, it has meaning,
Forever the awakened state –
Great bliss without samsaric reference.

Phenomena are empty of intrinsic nature
But the mind that holds to emptiness
Dissolves into its own ground.
Freedom from conceptual activity
Is the path of buddha?

I've put together these lines
That they may last for aeons to come.
By their virtue, may all beings without exception
Abide in the great state of Mahamudra.

*This doha (in Sanskrit:* Doha kosha nama; *in Tibetan:* Doha mdzod) *was composed by Maitripa. It was translated into Tibetan by the Indian master Berotsana.*

# The Life of the Guru Tilopa

Namo Guru Deva Dakini / sama yama nusmara / sidhyam tuye!

To the indeterminate, all-embracing, *trikaya*
maturing the disciple's nine dramatic faces;
to the *trikaya* of the dakinis
the great lake upholding the lotuses of pure pleasure;
to the lord of beings, Tilopa of Auspicious Insight,
and to Naropa who overcame the twelve hardships:
my humble welcome to them.

To those whose *trikaya*-gem
is bound by the seal of ignorance,
the *trikaya* gem shall be fully revealed
by the key of dakini symbolism

By the wish-fulfilling gem of initiatory experience
the *dharmakaya* is introduced;
through the wish-fulfilling gem of dream
the sambhogakaya resides in the body
and through the wish-fulfilling gem of lineage
the sambhogakaya is shown in manifestation.

The dakini-transmission is like the sun's radiance,
an expression that terrifies eclipsing the titan Rahu;
For the sake of my son Dode, I write these words,
and I pray with forbearance for the Dakinis blessing.

The Dakini's whispered instruction is not revealed to all:
although ravenous, who eats their parents' flesh?
although profitable, who sells deadly poison as food?
although a fantastic show who reveals heart-essence?

Three attributes are requisite for the display of this wonderful Dakini
Whispered Teaching: attributes of the teacher, the student,

and the essential teaching. The teacher's attributes are meditative experience and realisation in a compassionate lineage. The disciple's attribute is the potential for buddha to arise in his mind in this lifetime and in this body. The attribute of what is taught, the natural state of phenomena, has three aspects: externally it is the nirmanakaya instruction upon super activity and is called the Wish-fulfilling Gem of the Lineage; internally, it is the sambhogakaya instruction on meditative experience which is called the Wish-fulfilling Gem on the Path of Maturation; and in secret, it is the initiatory sambhogakaya instruction that is called the Wish-fulfilling Gem on the Path of Liberation.

Here is revealed the external aspect of the attribute of the teaching of the Dakini Whispered Transmission, which is nirmanakaya instruction, the Wish-fulfilling Gem of Lineal Transmission. In this section are the legends of the Dharmakaya Pure-Awareness Dakini and the legends of the nirmanakaya siddha lineage. As to the first, just as all buddha abides in the three modes of buddha-being so do the Pure-Awareness Dakinis, and this will be explained below in detail. As to the second, the first amongst the biographies of the lineage of the nirmanakaya siddhas is the life of Tilopa and it is divided into four parts. First, Tilopa's renown as a human being; second, as an emanation of Chakrasambara; third, as Chakrasambara himself; and fourth, as the essential body of all buddha.

## *Part One: Tilopa as a Human Being*

When this great lord Tilopa performed as a human being, four buddha-actions of his vast person are counted under two headings. The first heading is relative reality: 1) he received prophetic indications from the Dakinis, sought his gurus, and accomplished his sadhana; and 2) outshining the Dakinis, he requested their teaching; and then under the second heading, ultimate reality, he taught 3) that he had no human teacher; and 4) he showed various magical illusions.

*Chapter One: Dakini Indications, Finding the Teacher, and Attaining Siddhi.*

In Eastern India, in the land of Zahor, in the city of Jako, lived a brahmin named Selwa, Clarity, his wife called Selden, Radiance, together with their daughter called Selwai Dronma, Radiant Lamp. The couple were childless, so they made offerings to all the inner and outer supports of worship and their prayers were answered and a son was born. At that time Eastern India was bathed in light so the baby boy was named Selwo, Clear Light. The brahmin astrologer made this reading:

'Do not ask whether this baby is
god, serpent, demon or buddha,
But carefully cherish this remarkable being.'

The child was treated accordingly, and once when his father was absent and mother and son were left alone, out of an alternately shining and fading and multiplying vision an ugly crone, gasping, leaning on a stick, appeared. The mother thought that this must be a demoness and portend the death of her son, but the crone spoke:

'You may cherish the child
But nowhere is safe for him.'

'Then what can be done?' cried the mother.

'Let him herd the buffaloes and learn to read,
and wait for the Dakinis' indications.'

So saying the crone vanished.

The boy grew up and was allowed to tend the buffaloes. Once when he was out with the animals the same old crone appeared to him and asked him where he was from and who were his parents and so on. The boy replied:

'My land is Jako in the East;
My father is the brahmin Selwa, Clarity;
My mother is the brahmini Selden, Radiance;
My sister is Clear Lamp, Selwai Dronma;
I am the brahmin Clear Light, Selwo.
In this forest of aloe trees

I am learning to read the scriptures
and I guard these valuable buffaloes.'

The crone pretended to be angry telling him that he was completely ignorant. She said:

'Your country is Uddiyana in the East,
your father is Chakrasambara,
your mother is Vajra Varahi,
your sister is the Dakini Giver-of-Pure-Pleasure,
your name is Panchapana.

Do not herd animals
in this forest of bodhi trees,
but foster meditation experience.'

'I don't know how,' the youth responded.

'Then go to the Salabandha Cremation Ground and you will receive instruction from the Guru,' the crone predicted.

Then the youth went South to the Salabandha Cremation Ground, which was blessed by Maheshvara, where both outer and inner Dakinis turned the wheel of the dharma.

There he requested and received instruction from Krisnacharya, and the Mahacharya Lawapa sang to him:

'At a crossroads of a great city
I slept for twelve years
and attained Mahamudra-siddhi.'

And Lawapa bestowed the transmission of clear light upon him.

Then while searching for Nagarjuna, the boy found the charya-yogin Matangi meditating in a forest hut.

'Nagarjuna has gone to teach the dharma to an apsara king.' Said Matangi. 'You, fortunate boy, will be my disciple.'

The youth offered Matangi a suitable gift and received initiation into the *Guhyasamaja-tantra* through an emanated mandala and then through instruction in the tantra he saw the nature of mind.

In a temple where Panchapana sat to recite the priest's *Eight Thousand Verse Prajnaparamita Sutra*, the Dakini Subhabhadri appeared to him as a woman and asked him if he understood what he was reading. When he admitted that he did not understand, she offered to teach him and then gave him instruction. She gave him the Hevajra and the Chakrasambara initiations and instruction in the tantras.

'This is Luipa's transmission,' she told him. 'You must meditate upon it.'

Then because the priest did not permit him to meditate, she told him to hang the *Eight Thousand Verse Sutra* on a rope out of a temple awning so that it dangled in the water beneath and in that way to meditate upon crazy wisdom, and that through her blessing there would be no damage to the Sutra. He did as she commanded and the Sutra was undamaged, but he was whipped as a madman. Then he meditated on the two stages (creative and fulfilment) the essence of all paths, the radiant vision of the undivided buddha-mind.

Panchapana was given further predictions:

'In the east, in the land of Bangala,
in the market place of Panchapana
is the brothel of the whore Bharima.
Serve her faithfully and purifying yourself
completing your task, you will attain siddhi.'

In due course the youth arrived at that place. At night he worked as a pimp, but by day he pressed sesame seed and received his Sanskrit name, Tilopa (Telopa), 'Sesame Seed Sadhu', which in Tibetan is Tildung Zhab.

Then he went with Bharima to the Kereli Cremation Ground where through the sexual yoga of the secret tantra he achieved satisfaction and final consummation at the end of the path.

Then, further, in the market place, pressing sesame seeds, Tilopa came close to achieving final Mahamudra-siddhi. At that time the city people saw him in different forms. Some saw him as a blazing fire, and some saw only his bone ornaments on fire. All of them requested teaching from him and he would say, 'Let the authenticity born in my mind enter your hearts, my disciples!' And at that they were instantaneously liberated.

The local king came to pay his respects to him riding an elephant, accompanied by his retinue. The brahmin youth and the yogini Bharima sang this vajra-song with the purity of Brahma:

'Everyone knows that oil is sesame-essence,
but ignorant of the chemistry
they don't know how to extract it.
Just so, authentic, innate, awareness
abiding in the minds of all beings
remains unrealised until directed by the guru.
Pressing the sesame and getting rid of the dross,
its essence, the oil, is extracted;
just so, informed by the guru
by means of symbols, like sesame oil,
essential *suchness* is revealed.
The undifferentiated essence of all objects is one!
Yes! The heart of the ineluctable matter,
the profound meaning, is now clear!
How wonderful!'

Thus they sang, and the entire assembly gained liberation, and the meaning of the song was revealed to them, and there was nothing redundant in that matter, no application of any antidote necessary to attain pure awareness, no stages and paths to traverse, and no objective at all to attain. And the guru showed it simply by conventional symbols.

'Who is your guru?' they enquired.

'My human gurus are
Nagarjuna, Krisnacharya, Lawapa

And Subhabhadri, the All-good Dakini,
The gurus of the four transmissions.'

The four sublime streams of the whispered transmission are Apparitional Body received from Nagarjuna, Dream Yoga from Krisnacharya, the Yoga of the Clear Light from Lawapa and the Yoga of the Mystic Heat from the Dakini.

*Chapter Two: Propitiating the Dakinis and Receiving Instruction*

Then again the old crone appeared to Tilopa, saying:

'The whispered transmission beyond words,
Resides in the immaculate Dakini!
Take the threefold wish-fulfilling gem!

'I do not know how!' Tilopa replied.

The crone chorus chanted:

'In Uddiyana, in the Temple of Fragrance,
with foresight and commitment
the fortunate one can get it if he wants it.'

'If you do exactly as we tell you, you will get it,' they further instructed. 'Take a crystal ladder, a jewel bridge and a stem of burdock and go to Uddiyana.'

Tilopa had no trouble in finding the ladder, the bridge and the burdock and set out for Uddiyana with them.

In the West, in Uddiyana, in the Temple of Fragrance, dwells the Dharmakaya Awareness Dakini who abides nowhere but only in the nondual space of uninterrupted contemplation. She is like the Queen. Around her the Sambhogakaya Dakinis of the Five Families conceal in their palace of jewels surrounded by moat, an iron wall and castellation, the three-fold wish-fulfilling gem in an inaccessible iron box sealed with seven seals. The Dakinis are like the queen's ministers. Outside the five Minister-Dakinis are the ravenous incarnate Karma-Dakinis of the *dharmakaya* who bestow siddhi on those who have faith and respect but who kill and devour faithless vow-breakers. They are like the gate-keepers.

The brahmin youth, arriving in the West, in Uddiyana, before the Temple of Fragrance, was greeted by the Karma-Dakinis of the nirmanakaya, who shook the earth and the sky with their howl:

'We are the incarnate Karma-Dakinis of the Nirmanakaya!
We delight in human flesh and revel in blood!'

And as they started forward the Brahmin youth replied:

'Even you most horrible Dakinis
Stir not a hair on my head!'

And through the yogic quality of Total Presence he overwhelmed them with his radiance, and overcome by his gaze of unshakeable body, confident speech and dauntless mind those Dakinis fainted away. When they revived from their faint they said:

'Oh, alas! Like moths immolated in a lamp
We tried to consume you but we ourselves are destroyed.
Lord, do whatever you will with us!'

'Let me enter,' said the youth. But the Dakinis replied:

'Lord, be kind to us.
We are like servants with no authority.
If we don't ask the ministers
they will eat our flesh and drink our blood.'

So then he targeted the Sambhogakaya Minister-Dakinis. They told him, 'You have some small power which has defeated us. You may come in.' He crossed the moat using his jewel bridge, scaled the wall with his crystal ladder and opened the door with his burdock stem. But the Dakinis told him adamantly:

'Horrible bodies, horrible speech,
holding fearful weapons,

we are the five orders of Sambhogakaya Dakinis
and we delight in devouring flesh and drinking blood.'

The youth replied:
'You bunch of horrible Dakinis
stir not a hair of my head!'

And he gazed at them and they fainted away. When they had recovered, he told them he wanted to go inside but the Minister-Dakinis said:

'We are just feeble ministers.
If we don't ask the queen
we'll suffer later.
Lord, please be kind to us.'

Then they entreated the Dharmakaya Dakini to allow him to enter and the youth went inside. The Awareness Dakini of the Sambhogakaya was surrounded by innumerable Dakas to her right and Dakis to her left. But the youth payed no homage and the retinue murmured:

'This one shows no respect to Bhagawati,
the mother of all the Buddhas.
We should subdue him.'

And they tried to overcome him. But Vajra Yogini, the Sambhogakaya Dakini, stopped them, saying,

'This is the father of all the Buddhas,
Chakrasambara himself.
Even a storm of thunderbolts would not harm him.'

The retinue pretended not to recognise him as Chakrasambara and asked him roughly who sent him, who he was, and what did he want. He replied:

'I am Panchapana.
My sister Sukhada sent me.

I came to teach vision, action and the fruit,
the Mahamudra samaya and the *Trikaya*-Gem.'

The retinue laughed raucously and shouted:

'The blind look but cannot see,
the deaf listen but cannot hear,
and an idiot speaks but cannot understand:
How false the devil's deceptions!'

But the master replied:

'When bad karma is spent,
false words are untenable:
No devil approaches, but only the Dakini's truth.'

Then the Awareness Dakini revealed symbols of the precious wish-fulfilling gem: an image of the buddha-body, syllables of buddha-speech, and a mudra, a symbolic gesture, of buddha-mind. And the brahmin youth said:

'From the secret treasury of the unitary body of
    appearances and emptiness
I entreat the ordinary wish-fulfilling gem;
from the secret treasury of ineffable speech
I entreat the wish-fulfilling gem of SAMAYA;
and from the secret treasury of a thought-free mind
I entreat the wish-fulfilling gem of mind's nature.'

The Awareness Dakini replied:

'For the ordinary wish-fulfilling gem
you need the key of experiential vision —
if you have no vision you cannot open it.

For the wish-fulfilling gem of SAMAYA
you need the key of profound transmission —
without that antidote you cannot open it.
For the wish-fulfilling gem of the nature of being

you need the key of profound insight –
Without realisation you cannot open it.

'The Dakini's secret passport is the heart-SAMAYA;
the darkness of ignorance removed by that lamp
    of pure awareness,
Here I have the key of visionary inspiration,
and that is Total Presence, spontaneously arising, self-illuminating.

The self-liberating sambhogakaya, the nature of mind,
unborn nature of everything that arises,
dawns as self-liberating Mahamudra;
Here I have the key of self-liberating SAMAYA.

Awareness retained without conceiving an object
not so much as a shred of apperception is generated
and that is the sambhogakaya, *suchness* itself:
Here I have the key to visionary experience.'

Then the Dharmakaya, Sambhogakaya and Nirmanakaya Dakinis sang this song together:

'You are our only father, Bhagawan,
The buddha Tilopa, protector of beings;
Sublime Pleasure, Chakrasambara,
You have received the Three Wish-fulfilling Gems.'

Then the Dakini gave him the oral transmission comprising the fifty-five-chapter root tantra together with the explanatory tantra. Then she said, 'If you want to accomplish my body strive in practice of the creative stage. To accomplish my mind as the matrix of my speech, strive in the fulfilment stage of Mahamudra. Now go to the Jewel-Crest Monastery and take care of your three disciples Naropa, Riripa and Kasoripa.' And the Dakini, the principal of the mandala, vanished. The Brahmin youth received the name Telo Prajnabhadra, Telo of Auspicious Insight. He said:

'I am a bird in the sky,
a soaring bird of clear-light mind,
a daka of unobstructed insight!'

The Sambhogakaya and Nirmanakaya Dakinis entreated him:

'You, fearless one, do as you will,
But please stay here for our sake.'

Tilopa replied:

'According to the master's instruction,
I, the yogin, to benefit my disciples,
Now go to Jewel-Crest Monastery.'

Then Tilopa left that place and on the road he received the disembodied Dakini's Ninefold Teaching. He heard this vajra-speech of disembodied Dakinis, like the Lotus Eaters' sweet song, as if arising out of the *dharmadhatu*:

Maturation and liberation loosen the knots of the mind;
to maintain samaya look into the mirror of your mind;
for tsalung energy-flow turn the wheel of poetry;
for pure pleasure apprehend the jewel of speech;
for Total Presence look at the light of pure awareness;
for immediate liberation depend upon Mahamudra;
samaya substances are warmed by the sun of realisation;
buddha-action is like cutting water with a sword;
for the one taste look into the externalised mirror.

Tilopa listened to these words arising out of emptiness and said:

Lady, you have shown me just how it is.
Placing the Formless Dakinis' secret in this
    temple, the illusory body,
you have made iron of ineffable speech.
Now this bird of clear-light mind will fly away.

And he went to the Adona Temple in the Jewel-Crest Monastery.

## TILOPA'S LIFE-STORY

*Chapter Three: No Human Guru*

Many people gathered around Tilopa and they attained siddhi and they would ask him, 'You received this teaching in the Temple of Fragrance. Who is your Guru?' And Tilopa would reply:

'I have no human guru –
My teacher is all-knowing *dharmakaya*!'

*Chapter Four: Demonstration of Diverse Emanation in Conversion*

Tilopa's magical conversion is described in eight episodes: converting a yogin, a Hindu extremist, an illusionist, a barmaid, a singer, a butcher, a nihilist and a sorcerer.

*The Kusali Yogin Matchless*
In the south of India there was a king who loved his mother so much that he would do anything at all to keep her happy.

'Whatever kindness you ask me, that I will do,' he told her.

His mother told him, 'Assemble the pandits, siddhas and dakinis and have them make a vast mandala in the sky and perform initiation rites and a ganachakra feast. Then I will be happy.'

The king sent messengers to all the panditas and siddhas to invite them to such an event. They all duly arrived and a pandita performed the rituals of earth-consecration and so on and everyone was happy. Then a crone appeared before the Kusali-yogis and asked them who would preside over the ganachakra feast. A yogin called Matchless offered to preside, but the crone declared that her brother who lived in the cremation ground would challenge him for that privilege. Matchless agreed that he should be summoned for a contest. So it was that the crone's brother, Tilopa, arrived, and two thrones were erected.

First the two debated the proofs of the contrary teaching on language and meaning and they were equal in that. Then they both drew mandalas in the sky that were proof against rain and wind, and in that they were also equal. Then riding on lions they raced to the sun and moon and in that they were equally matched. Tilopa, in play, then made the sun and moon fall to the ground, and he rode upon them on the lion, and he turned his body inside out, and he emanated a cremation ground mandala in each of his body-hairs and in each cremation ground he emanated a tree and under each tree he was sitting in meditation.

Matchless could not perform such magical illusion. 'How wonderful!' he said. How do you do such magic? How do you perform such amazing activity?'

Tilopa sang this song:

'Wherever I sit, I sit at the centre of the sky,
wherever I sleep, I sleep on the tip of a spear,
wherever I gaze, I gaze at the centre of the sun and moon.
I am Tilopa who has ultimate realisation
free from all endeavour.'

Demonstrating the inconceivable nature of all things, Tilopa liberated beings. Matchless was renamed Nuden Lodro and he lived on in Uddiyana in a deathless state.

*The Hindu Extremist*
Once a Hindu Extremist, teacher and siddha, came to teach the assembly at Glorious Nalanda. Everyone, Buddhist and Hindu, was asked to rise in his presence, otherwise they must contest him in power and logic. When Tilopa refused to rise, the Hindu said:

'You are impatient to contend with me in debate and an exhibition of power. Let us begin.'

So with the king presiding, the Hindu and Buddhist panditas assembled. All would convert to the doctrine that proved superior in debate. The Hindu was not only defeated but could not withstand Tilopa in a subsequent contest of magical power. Then breathing fire the Hindu said:

'I can shake the three worlds at once.
Who are you who have no fear of me?'

Moving away from him, Tilopa sang:

'When I gaze, I gaze like a blind man;
when I am thirsty, I drink the water of mirage;
when I sink, I fill my stomach with wind.
Free from all fear, I am Tilopa.'

In that way Tilopa showed the inconceivable nature of reality, and everyone who heard him attained liberation. The Hindu magician was renamed Nakpo Gewa, the Virtuous Black, and he remained, deathlessly, in Sitavana, the Cool Grove Cremation Ground.

*The Illusionist*
Once when an illusionist threatened the kingdom with a magical army, a crone appeared in the principal city. She sought the king's general, and after meeting him she told the people that he was incapable of defeating the enemy. Only her brother was able to bring victory, she told them. They asked her where was her brother:

'In a cremation ground a mile from here, he has attached a horse tail to an aloe tree and to the horse tail he has tied a hand and foot of a human corpse and clutching the corpse he is swinging and dancing.'

This story was told to the king.

'The crone has told three lies. Bring her here!' he said.

The crone was brought before the king but she told the same story. Someone was sent to verify her tale and found it was as she said.

Tilopa was then invited to the city by the king and just as his army, ignorant of *maya*, was about to slip away, Tilopa destroyed the illusory host and some were killed and the illusionist was apprehended. He complained:

'You who follow the buddha-dharma,
how can you kill in this manner?'

And Tilopa replied:

'To kill an illusory army is no sin
because the army has no sentience.
When I kill, I kill only illusory beings,
when I meditate, I meditate beyond respiration,
when I speak, I speak with the tongue of the dumb,
when I assert the nature of reality, no words suffice.'

Tilopa sang the nature of inconceivable reality, and all attained liberation. The illusionist was renamed Luje Denma, Truth-Saying Deceiver, and he remained deathlessly in Haha Drokpa.

*The Barmaid*
Once when he found a barmaid selling liquor, Tilopa emanated a monkey and a cat who drank her liquor pots dry. The barmaid sobbed, and when her customers asked her the reason she told them what happened. 'Solicit the yogi!' they advised and tearfully she said to Tilopa:

'I have lost my livelihood!
Please be kind to me!'

Instantly the vats were again filled with liquor. Tilopa sang:

'When I drink, I drink boiling poison,
when my mind is dispersed, I chase and kill the monkey.
The antidote is reliance on the cat-yogin
and all is transformed into the innate one-taste.
I am the vagabond, Tilopa, an invisible yogi!'

Tilopa expressed inconceivable pleasure and all attained liberation. The barmaid was renamed Nyiwo Dronma, Lamp of Sunlight, and she dwelt deathlessly in Sosaling.

*The Singer*
Tilopa once met an accomplished singer and thought he would sing and challenge the singer to a contest. He suggested that the singer sing first and he after. The singer sang as long as he could and then

stopped. Then Tilopa sang and sang and did not stop. The singer gave him the victory and said:

'I am a master-singer who humbles
even Brahma's world. Who are you?'

Then Tilopa sang:

'When I suffer, I gaze at the Lotus-Eaters' city,
when I listen, I can hear the bees' song,
when I gaze, I can see with the eye of the blind:
The sounds I hear are just like echo.'

Tilopa demonstrated the inexpressible sound of music and all attained liberation. The singer was renamed Yangden Kukpa, The Melodious Mute, and dwelt deathlessly in Nagara (Pataliputra).

*The Butcher*

There was a butcher who killed animals' offspring to nourish his son. Once when he was boiling meat to feed his son, he lifted the lid from the pot and, through Tilopa's magic, he found his son's arms and legs inside. He cried:

'Is this the effect of my actions
returned to afflict me, or what?'

Miserable in his pain, Tilopa told him that if he stopped killing, his son would be returned to him. At that the butcher vowed he would never kill again.

Tilopa sang him this song:

'When cleaning, I separate the essence from the dross,
when cooking, I burn with millennial fire,
when turning out, I eject mind through the fontanelle,
when washing, I clean the mind's defilements.'

Tilopa expressed inconceivable slaughter and all attained liberation. The butcher was renamed Deje Gawa, Blissful Joy, and dwelt deathlessly in Shrimpo Ling.

*The Nihilist*

There was once a materialist who denied cause and effect, and claimed that virtue and vice did not exist. He argued with a Buddhist who asserted that they did exist. They called upon Tilopa to judge the case and the master, affirming that virtue and vice existed gave the Buddhist the victory in the argument.

The materialist said he did not understand the reason, so Tilopa, through magical emanation led him to the heavens and the hells. In one heaven the nihilist saw a solitary goddess, and asked why she was alone. Tilopa told him that some Hindu women practised virtue in order to obtain a husband. Then he led him to a hell where there were many cauldrons in which something boiled and one empty cauldron. When the materialist asked what was cooking in the full cauldrons, Tilopa told him that extremists who denied karma and virtue and vice were boiled there. The materialist was alarmed and said:

'Karmically gathered virtue
turns in the mind to heaven;
karmically gathered vice
turns in the mind to hell.'

Tilopa sang:

When I lust, I resort to a cremation ground island,
where I sink to the tip of the victory banner:
thought is emanation body –
I showed you nothing at all.

Tilopa showed inconceivably diverse emanation and everyone who saw attained liberation. The materialist was renamed Dzina Jangchub and dwelt deathlessly on Sriparvata.

Furthermore, through physical expression Tilopa taught the path to various miscreants – to an artisan, a yogi-sadhaka, and in the same way to a fisherman, a hunter and so on. Each of them said, 'You are a fisherman!' 'You are a hunter!' and so on. He replied:

'I am Tilopa who has ultimate realisation.
Virtue and vice do not exist for me.'

*The Sorcerer*
Once there was a sorcerer who through his magical power caused many people to die. When Tilopa saw that the time was ripe to convert him, he challenged him to a contest in killing. They performed equally in that, but then Tilopa resurrected all those whom he had killed except some of the sorcerer's women. 'You look like an old tree trunk!' Tilopa told him. 'If I resurrect the women will you cease from sorcery?'

Yet unrecovered the sorcerer said:

'Surely this irreversible activity
Is no different from the butcher's work.'

Then Tilopa sang this song:

'Look! Look at your own mind!
Swallow the mountain of appearances
and quaff at a gulp the vast ocean!
Bring the problem of samsara to final resolution.'

Tilopa showed inconceivable activity and everyone who saw him attained liberation. The sorcerer was renamed Nyimi, Sun-Man, and dwelt in Kimi Tsikili.

## *Part Two: Tilopa as an Emanation of Chakrasambara*

In the east of India in Nadukata, on the banks of the river Khasu, in the cremation ground Wounded-Flesh Grove, Mashe-Tsel, was a monastery called Asoka, No-Misery. The abbot and teacher were Tilopa's uncle and mother. Tilopa was ordained there as the bhiksu Kalapa. His fellow monks were assiduous in their study of the three levels of teaching, but Kalapa did not practice dharma, instead he would spend his time killing grasshoppers, plucking their heads from their bodies. Everyone censured him for this. The custodian of discipline called a supreme council of external monks and monks from the Asoka Monastery, which was presided over by the king. The king enquired:

'You look like a monk but you kill insects. Who is your abbot and master?'

Kalapa answered:

'My monastery is Ashoka, No-Misery,
my abbot and master are my uncle and mother,
I am the bhiksu Tilopa.
Thousands of years ago
I visited a hundred buddha-fields
and spoke with Nagarjuna,
Aryadeva and other buddhas,
And I saw the thousand buddhas.
I cannot kill sentient beings.'

Then it is said that the grasshoppers again began to buzz and fly away. Everybody believed his story and Kalapa became renowned as an emanation of Chakrasambara.

## *Part Three: Tilopa as Chakrasambara Himself*

Tilopa journeyed to the East begging alms. Begging in the street, his pace was correct and even, his gaze on the ground two yards ahead, and he uttered verses of sweet mantra. Returning, he uttered verses of thanks for what he had received. For this the people gave him every respect and the king invited him, together with other monks, to his palace. After paying his respects, the king said:

'All of you should recite verses of thanksgiving that are in harmony with the language of the grammarians, in accord with logic and the scriptures and precepts and meditation experience, and with the concepts of realised beings.'

Then all the monks recited verses, one after other, each in accord with the one before. When it was the master's turn his verses were in harmony with all the others that had preceded him and showed the ultimate meaning of all of them.

Later when the king questioned him, he replied:

I have no father or mother –
and Chakrasambara is supreme pleasure;
I have no abbot or teacher –
I am buddha self-sprung;
I have no grammar or logic –
my reason is an outflow of knowledge;
Sambara's Body Speech and Mind
are inseparable from my own body, speech and mind.
I have attained Pure Pleasure.

After saying that he became renowned as Sambara himself.

## *Part Four: Tilopa as the Essence of the Buddhas of Time*

King Singhachandra invited many siddhas to his city and gave them respect and homage and requested initiation. After Tilopa had made a mandala of coloured powder in the sky, people's vision of him varied and he sang this song:

'My body is Hevajra,
my speech is Mahamaya,
my mind is Chakrasambara,
aggregates and sense fields are Guhyasamaja,
my limbs are Krisnayamari,
my minor parts are Vajrabhairava,
and the hairs of my body are all buddhas.'

After singing that song Tilopa became renowned as the essence of all buddhas.

By the end of Tilopa's life the people of Zahor in the east attained maturation and liberation so that seven hundred thousand villages were emptied.

*This is the story of the Maheshyogi Tilopa, who attained siddhi and became renowned as a buddha-emanation. The activities of this great being were written down in a variety of texts. Here they are brought together as one. In the glorious gompa of Drowolung I have completed this composition for the sake of my son Dode.*

This colophon provides no author, but the author reveals himself as the father of Dode, who we take as Darma Dode, the son of Marpa Chokyi Lodro. Marpa was the root of the Kahgyu school of Buddhism in Tibet. His teacher was Tilopa. The Tibetan text has Telopa which has been amended as Tilopa.

# Appendix

## Nagarjuna's Twenty Mahayana Verses

Welcome to Manjusrikumarabhuta!

1. I bow down to the all-powerful buddha
The mind that is free of attachment,
Who in compassion and wisdom
Shows the inexpressible.

2. In truth no birth ever happens –
So surely no cessation or liberation;
Buddha is like the sky
And all beings have that nature.

3. Neither samsara nor nirvana exist,
But all is a complex continuum
With an intrinsic face of emptiness,
The object of ultimate awareness.

4. The nature of things
Appears like reflection,
Pure and naturally quiescent,
*Suchness* the nondual identity.

5. Common mind imagines a self
Where nothing at all exists,
And it conceives emotional states –
Happiness, suffering, and equanimity.

6. The six states of being in Samsara,
The happiness of heaven,
The suffering of hell,
Are all false creations, figments of mind.

7. Likewise, the notion that action causes suffering,
Old age, disease and death,
And the idea that virtue leads to happiness,
Are mere ideas, unreal notions.

8. Like an artist frightened
By the devil he paints,
The sufferer in Samsara
Is terrified by his imagination.

9. Like a man caught in quicksand
Thrashing and struggling,
Sentient beings drown
In the mess of their own thoughts.

10. Mistaking fantasy for reality
Causes suffering;
Mind is poisoned by interpretation,
Consciousness of form.

11. Dissolving figment and fantasy
With a mind of compassionate insight,
We must remain in perfect awareness
To help suffering beings.

12. Acquiring conventional virtue
Freed from the web of interpretive thought,
We gain unsurpassable understanding
As buddha, friend to the world.

13. Knowing universal relativity,
Ultimate truth is always visible;
Dismissing beginning, middle and end
The flow is seen as Emptiness.

14. All samsara and nirvana is seen as it is –
Empty and insubstantial,
Naked and changeless,
Eternally quiescent and illumined.

15. Just as the figments of a dream
Dissolve upon waking,
So the confusion of Samsara
Fades away in enlightenment.

16. Idealising things of no substance
As eternal, substantial and satisfying,
Shrouding them in a fog of desire
The round of existence arises.

17. The nature of beings is unborn
Yet beings are commonly conceived to exist;
Both beings and their ideas
Are false beliefs.

18. It is nothing but an artifice of mind
This birth into an illusory becoming,
Into a world of good and evil action
With good or bad rebirth to follow.

19. When the wheel of mind ceases to turn
All things come to an end;
Nothing is inherently substantial
And all things are utterly pure.

20. This great ocean of samsara,
Full of delusive thought,
Can be crossed in the boat 'Great Approach'.
Who can reach the other shore without it?

*Colophon*
The Twenty Mahayana Verses, *(in Sanskrit,* Mahayanavimsaka; *in Tibetan:* Theg pa chen po nyi shu pa) *were composed by the master Nagarjuna. They were translated into Tibetan by the Kashmiri Pandit Ananda and the Bhiksu translator Drakjor Sherab.*

From internal evidence these stanzas appear to be from the era of the Mahamudra siddhas and thus attributable to the siddha Nagarjuna rather than the first century AD Mahayana philosopher. But without more evidence I have refrained from including them in the main body of the book. The mahamudra-siddha Nagarjuna was a teacher of Tilopa.

FINI

Printed in Great Britain
by Amazon